exhibition album

Picasso
sculptor

exhibition organized by the Musée national d'art moderne/
Centre de création industrielle
with the Musée national Picasso,
on display at the Centre Pompidou,
from June 8 to September 25, 2000

Centre
Pompidou

Picasso sculptor

"An object! So my bird is not a sculpture [...] Who is going to tell me, Picasso, what is or isn't a sculpture! What is sculpture? What is painting? People hang on to old ideas as if the artist's role weren't precisely to create new ones[1]."

1. Picasso cited by Brassaï, *Conversations avec Picasso*, Paris, Gallimard, 1964. (English trans.: *Picasso and Company*, Garden City, N.Y., Doubleday, 1966, and London, Thames and Hudson, 1967.)

(cover)
Head of a Woman
1931
(reproduced p. 29)

**Picasso during the shoot
of the Georges Clouzot
film, "Le Mystère Picasso"**
1955, Nice
Photo Edward Quinn
Musée Picasso, Paris
Photo RMN/D. Arnaudet, Paris

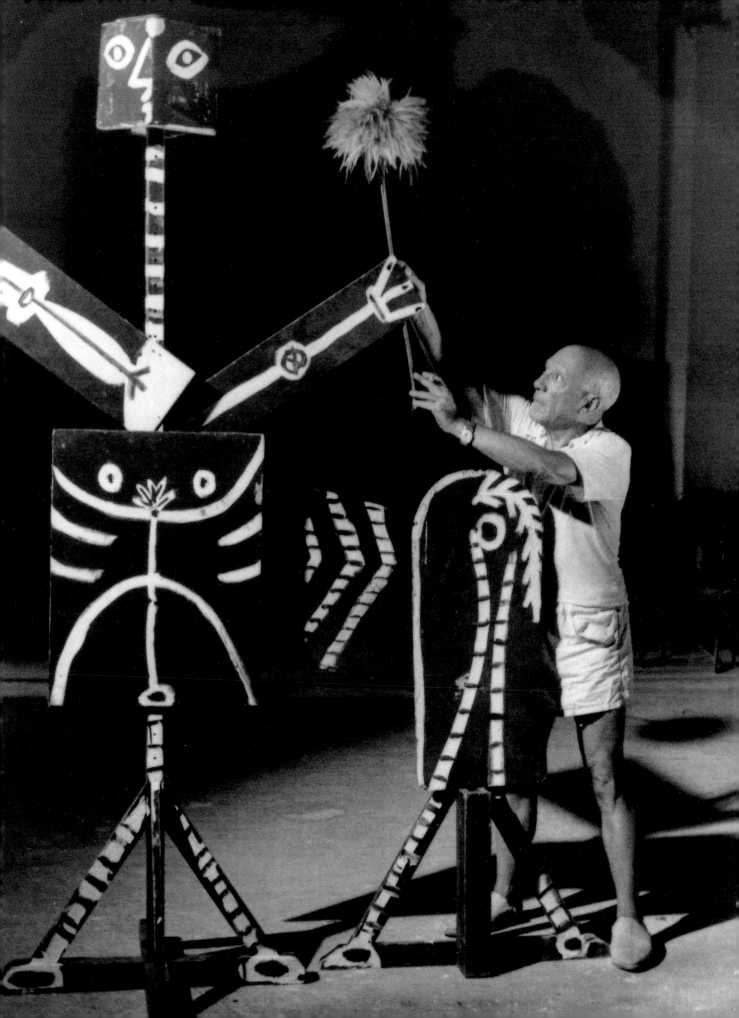

Picasso set out to wrest art away from the confines and conventions of representation, shattering taboos with his bold innovations and blazing new paths without necessarily exploring them himself. His insatiable curiosity pushed him to experiment over and over again and to take countless risks, and he was as stimulating to those who criticized him as he was to his admirers. He forged his own style by drawing on both tradition and contemporary forms of expression, making a decisive breakthrough, particularly in the field of sculpture – Picasso's "best-kept secret" for years. In his lifetime, no original sculpture left his homes or studios; he always kept the living proof of his creative spirit. Picasso's works surprised, amused, provoked and sometimes shocked. He saw them as having a kind of magical power, and, like an alchemist, kept them hidden away in the deepest recesses of his studio[2].

2. The first retrospective devoted to Picasso took place in the Galeries Georges Petit, in 1932, and presented only seven works; it was not until 1966 and 1967 that sculptures were presented to the public in Paris, London and New York.

Picador With a Broken Nose
1903
Plaster
18.5 x 13 x 11
Private collection
Courtesy Jan Krugier, Dittesheim
& Co, Geneva

Picasso didn't actively begin to focus on sculpture until 1902 and 1903, with *Sitting Woman*, *Blind Singer*, and *Picador With a Broken Nose*. In 1905, two works followed that featured softer contours: *Female Head (Alice Derain)*, and *The Jester*, underscoring the link between painting and sculpture, as Picasso used themes often depicted in his paintings: tumblers and acrobats. Each week, he went to the Médrano Circus with friends, and was fascinated by the spectacle. Coming home from the circus one evening, Picasso did a portrait of his friend Max Jacob, but he modified the head, and only the lower part of the face reproduced Jacob's features. This gave it the appearance of a circus performer. The *Head of a Woman (Fernande)* that followed, in 1906, is certainly interesting in its asymmetrical composition of the face, but like the others, was part of a group of works which was neither very significant nor very audacious. Rodin's influence can be felt in these works. Picasso had seen the works in the Rodin pavilion on the Place de l'Alma on his first trip to Paris in 1900, as well as those of Medardo Rosso and of Bourdelle.

The Jester
1905, Paris
Bronze
41.5 x 37 x 22.8
Musée Picasso, Paris
Photo RMN/B. Hatala, Paris

In 1906, Picasso made a breakthrough in his sculpture: the discovery of the African statue bought by Matisse, and the trip to Gosol, a small village in the Catalan mountains, caused a profound mutation in his art. The first examples were the carvings, a technique already used by Gauguin, whose work he knew since 1901 but the technique had grown obsolete by the twentieth century. The retrospective exhibition devoted to Gauguin – one of the first artists fascinated by exotics – in the Salon d'Automne in 1906, pushed him to realize a series of impressive and monumental totemic figures, completed in 1907. They are contemporary to the *Demoiselles d'Avignon*, and have the same brutality and a similar geometric simplification of the volumes. Their bodies are blocks with breasts and belly protruding, similar to the tikis from the Marquesas Islands that Picasso owned. We can find in all these figures the posture of Polynesian statuettes with their slightly bended legs. The *Figure* carved in boxwood evokes however Iberian sculpture, especially the *Dame d'Elche*. Kahnweiler later made a crucial remark concerning this period: "For the true discovery of African and Oceanic art to take place, it had taken Picasso's preliminary studies for the *Demoiselles d'Avignon* to create the proper climate in the autumn of 1906[3]." Kahnweiler's statement corroborated Picasso's own comments emphasizing that the primitive statues he owned were testimonies more than examples, and asserting that he had discovered the collection of the Ethnographic Museum at Trocadero in Paris only in the summer of 1907, even if, on occasion – as seen in the sketchbooks – he was inspired by various African pieces.

3. Daniel-Henry Kahnweiler, *Juan Gris, sa vie, son œuvre, ses écrits*, Paris, Gallimard, 1946.

Figure
1907
Shaped boxwood bearing traces
of crayon; top of head painted
35.2 x 12.2 x 12
Musée Picasso, Paris
Photo RMN/B.Hatala, Paris

In the autumn of 1909, he made a major breakthrough with *Head of a Woman* in deconstructing the head of his companion, Fernande Olivier, using alternating concave and convex surfaces. One can only note the strangeness of his re-creating in *ronde-bosse* the portraits painted the previous summer in Horta de Ebro. The forms have been decomposed and the features, particularly the forehead, are rendered as facets, which had been justified in the paintings in that such fragmentation was necessary on a two-dimensional surface. The *ronde-bosse*, which can be looked at from all angles, allows the work to be grasped as a whole: the process of decomposition by facets becomes either merely an artist's whim or the desire to introduce Cubist stylization of painting into the sphere of sculpture. While the aspect of a traditional bust is retained, Fernande's head is chaotic, with its projections and hollows capturing and diffusing the light, introducing a discontinuity in the representation of volume unexplored until then. This daring principle was to be taken up and used by numerous sculptors over the course of the twentieth century. In 1912, Picasso and Braque invented the collage, paper cut-outs and the constructions which represented a new formulation of reality: collages and paper cut-outs – newspaper, imitation-wood or marble wallpaper or flowered wallpaper, colored paper, music scores, labels of aperitif bottles, business cards, playing cards, packs of cigarettes – through the simplicity of their forms and flat colors enabled the reorganization of the space of the canvas or the drawing, which moved from plane to volume. At the same time, assemblages allowed objects to be considered as a sculptural art form for the first time. The Cubist assemblages or constructions are not completely three-dimensional, however, since they still acknowledge the plane of the wall by their frontality, the only *ronde-bosse* of the time being *Glass of Absinthe* (1914).

Head of a Woman (Fernande)
autumn 1909, Paris
Bronze
40.5 x 23 x 26
Musée Picasso, Paris
Photo RMN/B. Hatala, Paris

(following pages)
Glass of Absinthe
spring 1914, Paris
Sand and painted bronze,
spoon for absinthe
21.5 x 16.5 x 6.5
Centre Pompidou, Mnam-Cci,
Paris

Glass of Absinthe
1914, Paris
Painted bronze,
spoon for absinthe
21.6 x 16.4 x 8.5
The Museum of Modern Art,
New York
Gift of Mrs. Bertram Smith, 1956

The first sculpture assemblage was *Guitar*, though it is unclear whether the cardboard version preceded the metal version or vice-versa. Picasso was well aware of the novelty of *Guitar*, as his comment to André Salmon at the time reveals: "It's nothing, it's *el guitar*! There it is. The walls have come tumbling down. We are freed from painting and sculpture already liberated from the idiotic tyranny of genres. It is no longer this or that. It is *el guitar*[4]."

These objects belong neither to painting nor to sculpture. They are *tableaux-reliefs* halfway between plane and space where the background acts as a support from which the various elements escape in their conquest of space. In the spring of 1914, Picasso used tinplate for the first time; he used a can of powdered milk, which he cut up and painted, then bronzed, then painted again for *Bottle of Bass, Glass and Journal*. *Glass of Absinthe*, originally modeled in wax, exists in six copies. One has traces of sand, the five others are painted differently; Picasso answered Marcel Duchamp by asserting that the work of art was unique, even if – and especially if – he used a real absinthe spoon on which he placed an imitation sugar-cube. *The Violin* of 1915, a superimposition of colored planes stemming from the work on *papiers collés*, heralded another step : the transposition of the instrument's forms in the folded, cut-up and painted sheet metal were a departure from the imitative function of sculpture. It was an idea of a violin that was presented, no longer the object itself. *The Violin* became an abstraction, and the sign itself, which several years earlier had allowed the viewer to better grasp the Cubist configuration by conveying the whole of which it was only a partial element, ceased to be a signifier and even added to the confusion. The figures of the *Managers*, for the ballet *Parade* (1917) and the *Guitar* of 1924 constituted the swan song of Cubist constructions.

4. André Salmon, *La Jeune Sculpture française*, Paris, 1919.

Bottle of Bass, Glass and Newspaper
1914
Construction: cut-out, folded and painted tin, sand, wire and paper
20.7 X 14 x 8.5
Musée Picasso, Paris
Photo RMN/B. Hatala, Paris

Guitar
late 1912
Construction: cardboard, string and wire
66.3 x 33.7 x 19.3
The Museum of Modern Art, New York
Gift of the artist, 1973

(following pages)
Mandolin and Clarinet
autumn1913, Paris
Construction: fir components with paint and crayon strokes
58 x 36 x 23
Musée Picasso, Paris
Photo RMN/B. Hatala, Paris

Violin
1915, Paris
Construction: cut-out, folded and painted sheet-iron, and wire
100 x 63.7 x 18
Musée Picasso, Paris
Photo RMN/B. Hatala, Paris

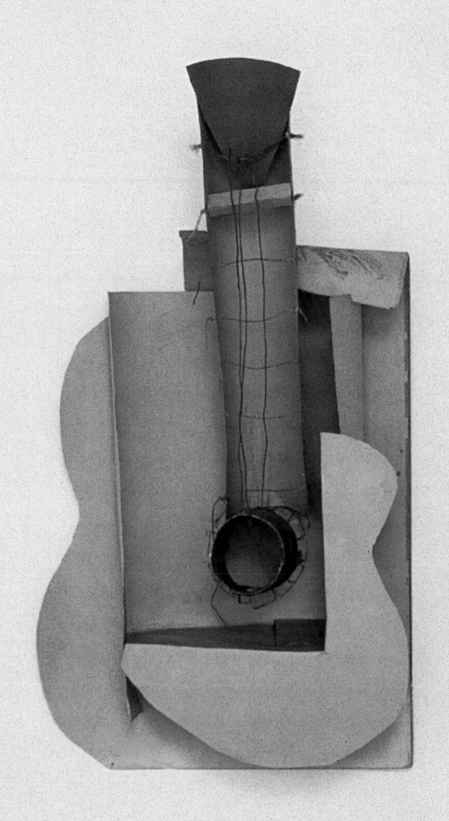

During the period spanning these two dates, Picasso left sculpture aside; it was sublimated in his painting by the representations of colossal women, nude or draped in the antique manner or in Greek profile, which haunt his work – references to the Greco-Roman statuary he had seen during his trip to Italy from February to May 1917: they are "Cow-eyed Juno whose massive broken hands hold up folds of stone[5]."

If sculpture was set aside for the most part during the 1920s, his paintings and sketchbooks were filled with figures and motifs conveying a desire to take up the discipline again. It was clear enough for Christian Zervos to note: "Picasso could be considered at certain moments of his œuvre as the artist par excellence whose paintings are often based on the particulars of sculpture and coincide with them. This is true for most of the works of the period that concern us. It can be said that there is not a painting of the time which is not touched by the spirit of sculpture or which does not have its counterpart in a sculpture[6]."

In 1928, Picasso proposed several projects for a monument to Guillaume Apollinaire; they were filiform constructions which resembled a kind of spatial calligraphy: "So full of fantasy and grace, so harmonious, so human, so personal, the work was done with such love and tenderness in memory of his dear friend that he no longer wants to let go of it, does not want to know that it is in Père-Lachaise cemetery, in that bazaar of monuments where people rarely ever go[7]."

5. Jean Cocteau, *Picasso*, Paris, Stock, 1923.

6. Christian Zervos, *Catalogue raisonné, Vol. VII (1926-1932)*, Paris, Cahiers d'Art, 1955.

7. Julio González, "Picasso et les cathédrales, Picasso sculpteur", *González-Picasso dialogue*, exhibition catalogue, Paris, R.M.N. /Centre Pompidou, 1999.

**Figure (suggested
as design for a monument
to Guillaume Apollinaire)**
autumn 1928, Paris
Wire and sheet-iron
50.5 x 18.5 x 40.8
Musée Picasso, Paris
Photo RMN/B. Hatala, Paris

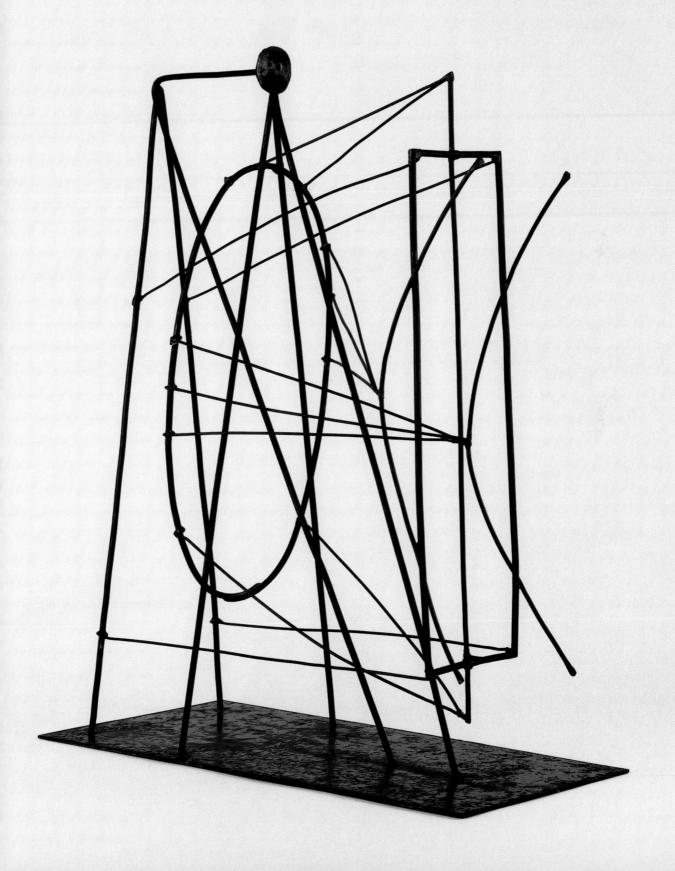

Julio González played a key role for Picasso in the soldered and painted iron works. *Woman in the Garden* (1929), revolving around void and transparency – key elements in his art at the time – is a fragile assemblage of steel rods and sheet-iron, carved, soldered then painted, composed of two complementary languages, that of planes and that of lines in space. One finds the recurrent motifs of the painting of the period: a woman, mouth full of teeth and streaming hair – the bean-shaped metal sheet endowed with breasts and the pierced orifice on the round sheet – inspired by the large philodendron leaves that Picasso had in his possession on Rue La Boétie. The *Head of a Woman* from 1929-1930, an assemblage of iron and sheet-iron to which Picasso added springs and colanders, is painted white. Paint plays a very important role in the assemblages, as it nullifies the qualities of the materials, canceling out the differences in color of the metal, which is not used for itself but as a support, as bronze would be used later on. The choice of white corresponds to the desire for lightness, for immaterialism, for a desire to distance sculpture from reality regardless of the presence of deliberately chosen objects, whose use is not the result of chance – quite the opposite: "I said to González: 'Buy me some colanders' and he brought me back two new colanders."

At the same time, Picasso's art was developing close ties with Surrealism and with its leader, André Breton, who recognized Picasso's creative genius without trying to make any claims for it: "Surrealism, if it is to assign itself a line of conduct, can then take the same path Picasso has taken and will take again; I hope that in saying this I am showing myself to be highly demanding. I will always be opposed to the idea that a label can impose an absurdly restrictive character on the activity of a man of whom we expect the most[8]."

8. André Breton, "Le Surréalisme et la peinture", *La Révolution surréaliste*, n° 4, 15 July 1925.

Head of a Woman
1929-1930, Paris
Painted iron, sheet-iron, springs
and colanders
100 x 37 x 59
Musée Picasso, Paris
Photo RMN, Paris

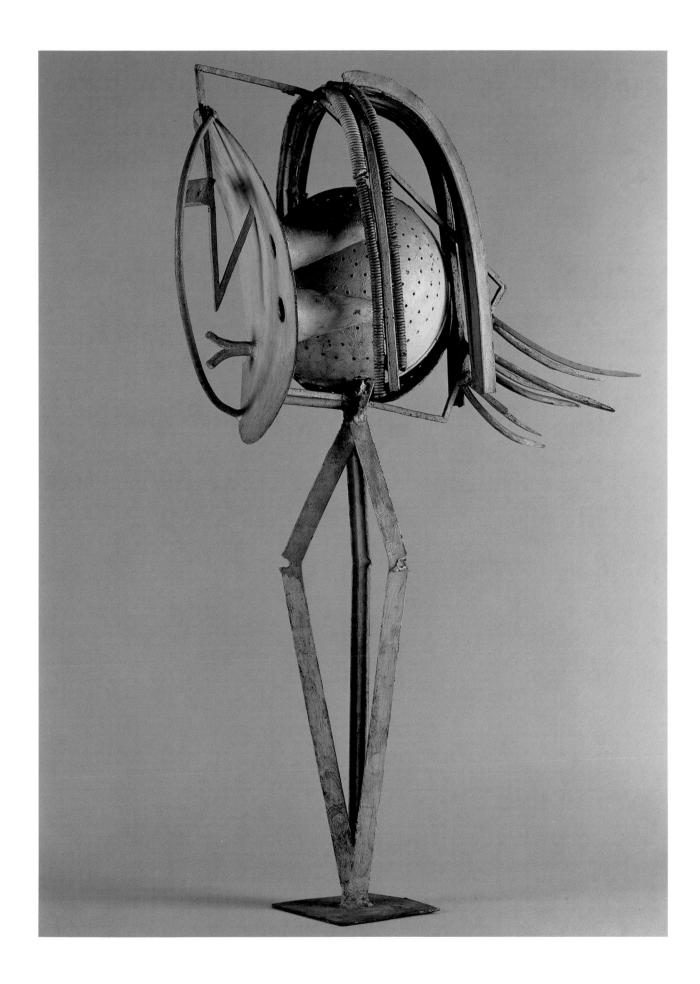

As of 1925, his painting and, a little later, his sculpture became a ground for transgressing taboos, whether artistic or moral. The sand-reliefs made in Juan-les-Pins in August 1930, in which Picasso juxtaposed small discarded objects often found at the beach on strolls, derived from Surrealist thought through their dream-like appearance, even if they lacked the automatic-writing characteristics of André Masson's sand paintings. He combined the strangeness of these small objects forgotten by vacationers or rejected by the sea, mixed with the seaweed he used for hair, with sand, which he projected onto the work, a uniform gray veil underscoring a sense of nostalgia or abandonment as if they were vestiges of a lost civilization. Heteroclite assemblages such as these stimulate the artist's imagination as much as the spectator's, suggesting the deep recesses of the conscience which often materialize in dreams or fantasies. Several lines written by Max Ernst come to mind: "The very absurdity of the assemblage unleashed a sudden intensification of my faculties as a visionary and gave birth to a hallucinatory series of contradictory images, double images, triple and multiple images superimposing over each other with the persistence and rapidness which are those of remembrances of love and half-sleep visions[9]."

9. Max Ernst, *Au-delà de la peinture. Histoire d'une histoire naturelle*, 1936.

**Composition
With a Butterfly**
*September 15, 1932, Boisgeloup
Cloth, wood, plants, string,
drawing pin, butterfly and oil
paint on canvas, 16 x 22 x 2.5
Musée Picasso, Paris
Photo RMN/B. Hatala, Paris*

Composition With a Glove
*August 22, 1930, Juan-les-Pins
Sand, stained in places, on back of
canvas and stretcher; glove, card-
board and plantspasted and sewn
on the canvas, 27.5 x 33.5 x 8
Musée Picasso, Paris
Photo RMN/B. Hatala, Paris*

"Remembrances of love and half-sleep visions": no words could better describe *Composition With a Glove*, in memory of the small Mediterranean town where Picasso spent the summer not only with his wife, Olga, but also with his young mistress Marie-Thérèse Walter, whom he had convinced to join him. The pretty sleeping girl with the minuscule head, whose cheek reposes on a disproportionate right hand, is lying on the sand. A round breast looms up from the seaweed, defining her as a woman or the dream of a woman, desire of a real or imagined evasion.

Two years later, Picasso glued matchsticks, a piece of cloth, plant fibers, a bit of string, a linden leaf and a butterfly onto a canvas coated with creamy white paint, the butterfly unfolding its wings for all eternity, unfazed by the brusque movements of the small figures. "It was in 1932 that, for the first time, a real butterfly was inscribed on the surface of the canvas. It was the first time that he was able to do it without everything around it crumbling to dust, without the overwhelming representations and its presence on this spot upsetting the system of human representations of which it was part[10]."

10. André Breton, "Picasso dans son élément", *Minotaure*, n° 1, 1933.

**Head of a Woman
in Profile (Marie-Thérèse)**
1931
Bronze
68.5 x 59 x 8
Musée Picasso, Paris
Photo RMN, Paris

Picasso was also a Surrealist through the violence and *débordements* that appeared in the series of *Guitars* in the spring of 1926, assemblages of discarded objects and old nails (he even thought for a moment of using razor blades). The guitar is a metaphor for the female body, hence the discomfort in seeing it pierced with nails, which also served to ward off anyone who would attempt to pick it up. Any sense of harmony or balance is excluded here. Picasso's reliance on instinct here seems to go hand in hand with Breton's motto: "Beauty shall be 'convulsive' or shall not be." Sculpture became the setting for metamorphosis. Picasso's plastic vocabulary reached new, innovative heights: the human body, in the early 1930s, was constructed through the interlocking or layering of spongy or mineral materials, creating bold erotic metaphors or explicitly evoking the rawness of sexual relations. *Metamorphosis II*, a small figure with tumescent forms, was seen as "a bizarre, monstrous, crazy, incomprehensible, almost obscene work, a sort of indescribable block with genitalia emerging here and there[11]." The encounter with the luminous, sensual Marie-Thérèse in 1927 explains Picasso's persistent focus on erotic themes, particularly present in the *Heads* done at Boisgeloup.

11. André Billy, cited by Paul Léautaud, *Journal littéraire*, tome 4, Paris, Mercure de France, 1954-1964.

Metamorphosis II
1928
Plaster original
23 x 18 x 11
Musée Picasso, Paris
Photo RMN/B. Hatala, Paris

In 1932, Brassaï discovered Picasso's new studio: "I would guess that when Picasso visited the estate for the first time, it wasn't the small chateau that seduced him as much as the vast empty rooms that needed to be filled up... He could finally satisfy a long-pent-up desire: to sculpt monumental statues. He opened the door to one of those vast rooms and we could see, in all their dazzling whiteness, a whole tribe of sculptures...[12] "

Picasso was bewitched by Marie-Thérèse, and began to concentrate primarily on nudes; he put his full energy into the study of the anatomy – that of the woman he loved, the incarnation of desire. The interplay of curves, undulating shapes, globular breasts, arching hips, and voluptuous buttocks of the *Bather Reclining* illustrate the pleasure of sensuality.

The nose of the large *Head of a Woman*, a work impressive in its whiteness, takes on a phallic, erectile aspect, its vaginal mouth promising pleasure and fertility. The eyes are incised in cheeks as thick as thighs, making the work a disquieting evocation of the Nimba mask from Guinea which Picasso had at Boisgeloup. The *Bather* (1932), with its head reduced to a conglomerate of folds and rolls, missile-shaped breasts, and deformed hips and thighs, is reminiscent of the *Venus of Lespugue*, of which he owned two copies.

12. Brassaï, *Conversations avec Picasso, op.cit.*

Head of a Woman (Marie-Thérèse)
Anonymous photograph
Boisgeloup, 1931
Musée Picasso, Paris
Photo RMN/F. Raux, Paris

Head of a Woman
1931
Plaster original: plaster and wood
128.5 x 54.5 x 62.5
Musée Picasso, Paris
Photo RMN/B. Hatala, Paris

Picasso's inventiveness found other spheres of activity at Boisgeloup, resulting in filiform figures carved in wood – *Woman With Foliage*, *Couple*, *Female Bust* – and assemblages. *Woman With Foliage* combines the imprint of corrugated cardboard made with plaster and that of a beech leaf, an example of Picasso's constant imaginative use of whatever materials were at hand: wood, plaster, steel wire, paper and metal, the latter allowing him to experiment with the randomness of modeling and assemblages. (Bronze casting does not permit the handiwork of the artist.) Dealers and friends urged him to tackle this problem, and he often "reappropriated" bronzes by painting them.

Picasso worked at Boisgeloup until 1935, when he and Olga divorced. His creativity suffered, and he turned away from the plastic arts for a certain period of time. He did not really return to sculpture until moving to the studio which his new companion, Dora Maar, had found for him on Rue des Grands-Augustins in Paris. This marked the beginning of a new artistic *élan* set against the backdrop of a world in conflict.

Figure
1935
Assemblage: ladle, claws, wood,
string and nails
112 x 61.5 x 29.8
Musée Picasso, Paris
Photo RMN, Paris

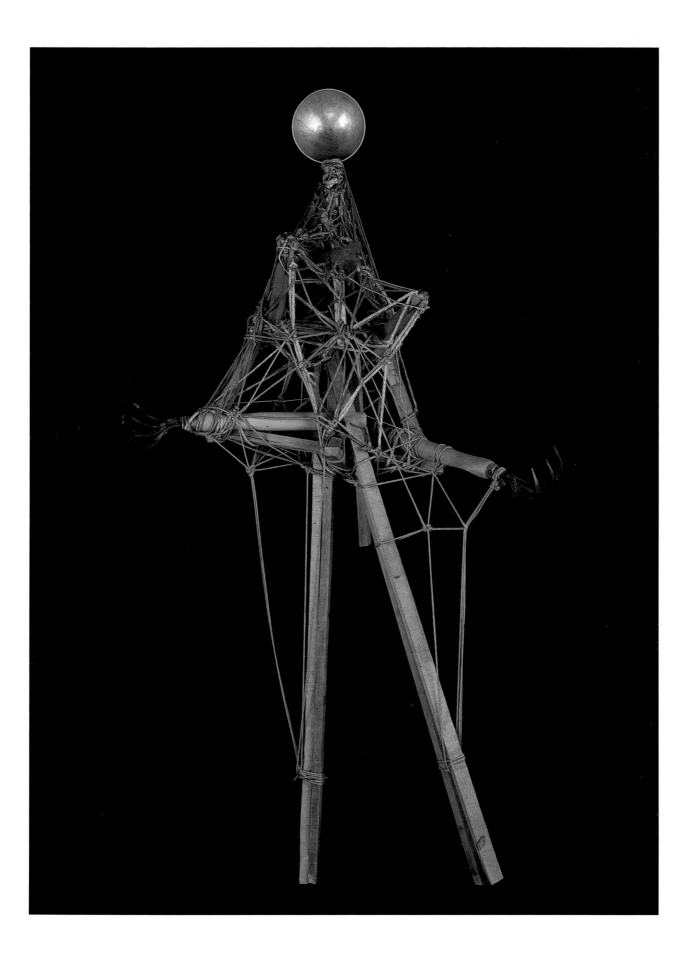

The few sculptures made during this period bear the marks of the war – the deprivation, mourning and tragedy. Picasso did not leave his studio the entire year of 1942, a period which was an important step in the practice of assemblages of objects taken from reality as with the *Head of a Bull*. "A metamorphosis has taken place, but now I would like a metamorphosis to take place in the opposite direction. Suppose that my bull's head was discarded and that one day a man arrives and says, ''Here's something that could be used as the handlebars for my bicycle''; in this way a double metamorphosis will have been achieved." The work was the result of the assemblage of two found objects: a bicycle seat and bicycle handlebars, everyday objects magnified by Picasso's poetic, resourceful vision; magic, playfulness and an homage as well to Julio González, who died on March 27. *Head of a Bull* was cast in bronze. Picasso marveled over bronze's bringing together the elements, yet stressed that "if one sees only the head, if the handle bars and the seat are no longer recognizable, the work loses its interest". The head was a *Vanitas* that found its counterpart in the *Death's Head* the following year, a gripping, tragic vision of human destiny, "a block of stone, hollowed out with recesses, corroded and polished from having rolled through the ages, " with its empty eyesockets, its nose eroded and its mouth gnawed away. Or perhaps the *Reaper* which, despite the solar aspect of the head, evoked for André Malraux an image of death, to the point that he had thought of erecting an enlarged version at the tip of Île Saint Louis in Paris as a monument to the poet Charles Baudelaire.

Head of a Bull
spring 1942
Original components: bicycle
saddle and handlebars (leather
and metal)
33.5 x 43.5 x 19
Musée Picasso, Paris
Photo RMN/B. Hatala, Paris

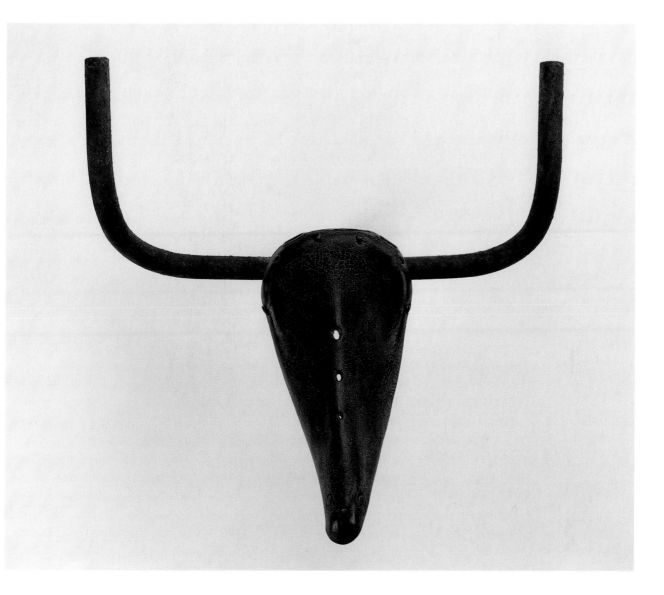

In contrast to this pessimism, *Man With a Sheep* (February or March 1943) became symbolic of hope and renewal, the surge the viewer's heart could not help but feel in glimpsing liberty at the end of the dark Hitlerian night shrouding Europe. "And Picasso designated me the Man with the lamb who, two meters high, dominates this population of statues... Naked, steady on his long skinny legs, his round head bald – his surly face looks like Ambroise Vollard's – the giant grasps a lamb in his powerful arms. The left hand grips the backbone as the heavy animal struggles, the right hand holds three of the four hooves, the fourth escaping his grip... It is modeled quite freely, with rapid lumps of clay, like certain large Etruscan terra cotta pieces. The *Man With a Sheep* seems to have been made in a single burst of creativity[13]." Far from having been made in a single burst of creativity, the sculpture was preceded by a great number of preparatory studies, proving once again that Picasso's apparent rapidity was in fact the fruit of many long months of work and thought; its origin dates back to mid-July 1942. The artist captured the position of the lamb very quickly, going from an animal peacefully curled up against the man's chest – the Good Shepherd? – to that of an animal clamoring to escape, through the stiffening of its body and the twisted and bleating movement of the head, to the implacable grip of the man who will offer it in sacrifice, the expiatory victim par excellence, whose death ensures our mercy. Picasso hesitated more in the depiction of the man or rather of his personalization: a beardless young man barely out of adolescence, a mature man with first a kind and then a brutal face, but in the end it is a bearded, bald, determined old man that is chosen to be worked in clay.

13. Brassaï, *Conversations with Picasso, op. cit.*

Man With a Sheep
February or March 1943
Bronze
222.5 x 78 x 78
Musée Picasso, Paris
Photo RMN, Paris

The making of the sculpture itself is quasi-miraculous: "I finished this statue in a single afternoon... Paul Eluard was there... I first erected the armature... But it is rarely calculated right... Mine was rather off the mark... Much too weak, it couldn't support the weight... The statue was starting to collapse under the weight of the clay. It was terrible! It could fall apart at any moment. Something had to be done quickly. I got Paul Eluard to help... We got ropes and hung the *Man With a Sheep* from the rafters. I decided to cover it with plaster then and there. We did it the same afternoon. What work that was! I won't forget it... I had intended to rework it... You see those long skinny legs, the flimsily sketched feet, barely off the ground; I wanted to model them like the rest. But I didn't have enough time. Finally, I had to leave it the way it was. Now it's too late. He is the way he is. If I touched it now, I could ruin everything[14]."

Picasso always denied the symbolic character of this sculpture: "It's not in the least religious. The man could just as well be carrying a pig as a sheep! There is no symbolism in it. It is just something beautiful... In *Man With a Sheep*, I expressed a human feeling, a feeling that exists today the way it always has[15]." Certainly, this is what he wanted to express in the work that greeted visitors to the studio on Rue des Grands-Augustins, like a statue of a Commander. But was it possible that the choice of such a theme evoking the death of Christ on the cross, the redemption of sins and the resurrection at the height of the war was purely by chance?

14. Brassaï, *Conversations with Picasso*, op. cit.

15. Picasso, "Permanence du sacré", *xxᵉ Siècle*, n° 24, December 1964.

Picasso in the Grands-Augustins studio, Paris, with "Man With a Sheep", plaster version
ca. 1944
Photo Robert Capa
Musée Picasso, Paris
Photo RMN, Paris

In addition to these dramatic figures of the war years, Picasso also did lighter, brighter works, some of which are based on Dora Maar: *Female Head* (1941), which in the first version in plaster bore an extravagant little hat and had a gentle, serene expression. The allegorical figure of the Muse, its bronze was placed in 1959 in the little garden next to the church at Saint-Germain-des-Prés in Paris as a monument to Apollinaire, and was stolen in 1998, one year after Dora's death – beloved Dora, for whom Picasso began making charming objects, in 1943, with paper napkins or paper restaurant tablecloths, or with Celtique cigarette packs, little tokens of their passion. Some saw the objects as heralding the sheet-iron sculptures which were so important in Picasso's last years as a sculptor; others saw them as intimate objects, like *Head of a Dog (The White Lap Dog)*, the image of the little toy dog whose death she deplored. Picasso offered this to her as a consolation.

Woman in a Long Dress (1943) stems from a wooden mannequin he found, to which he added a head and arms: "One day at the flea market, I came across a wonderfully-sculpted haute couture mannequin from the Belle Époque, with a high bust, an amply proportioned derriere, without arms or a head... So I gave it arms and a head... All I did was adjust them[16]." Picasso fashioned a jointed doll, which he later dressed in a white smock covered with paint, and gave a palette and a handful of paintbrushes. It was "the painter with his luminous, radiant palette". Paris was liberated on August 25, 1944, and the years following the war were full of joy rediscovered.

16. Brassaï, *Conversations avec Picasso, op. cit.*

Head of a Dog
(The White Lap Dog)
1943
Torn and burned cotton paper
(napkin)
10 x 27
Musée Picasso, Paris
Photo RMN, Paris

(following page)
The Grands-Augustins
studio with "Aubade" and
"Woman in a Long Dress"
1946
Photo Brassaï
Musée Picasso, Paris
Photo RMN/M. Bellot, Paris

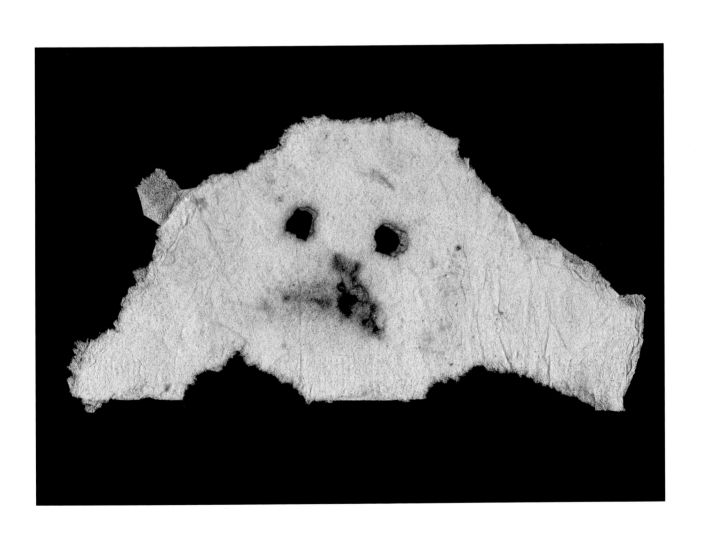

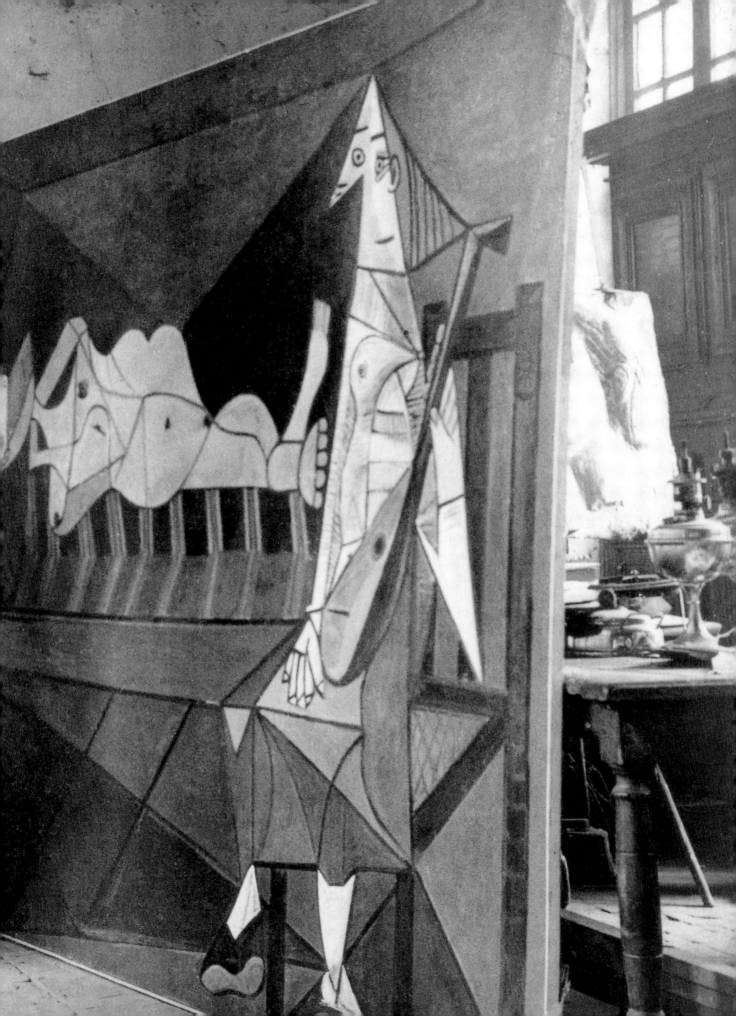

"You should think of ceramics. It's wonderful[17]!"

Picasso moved to Vallauris, a small potter's village, in 1947 with Françoise Gilot, and found a studio on Rue du Fournas. Here, he made his ceramics, which can be classified into two categories: on the one hand, the everyday objects, plates, vases and dishes, which were supports for his painting; and on the other, the pieces which are like sculptures, particularly the owls and the anthropomorphic vases. "It's quite similar but naturally there is the flowing enamels applied to the forms and the forms are colored, adding paint makes it a different object[18]."

17. Conversation between Picasso and Henri Laurens, cited by D.-H. Kahnweiler, *Picasso-Keramik, Hannover*, Fackelträge-Verlag, 1970.
18. Radio interview with Picasso by Jean d'Alvez in Vallauris, November 2, 1961.

**Picasso modeling
ceramics in Vallauris**
ca. 1947
Photo Pierre Manciet
Musée Picasso, Paris
Photo RMN, Paris

Picasso had met Georges and Suzanne Ramié in 1946, who ran a ceramics works in Vallauris, the Madoura studio. Picasso became passionately interested in this technique, making objects in the most haphazard way, which led the Ramiés to say that "an apprentice who worked like Picasso would never find a job". But, in the field of ceramics, Picasso shattered traditions once again, creating highly inventive works full of verve and imagination. The comical nature of the sculptures corresponds to the gracefulness of the ceramics. Picasso used whatever he found at hand: a jar, toy cars – his son Claude's Panhard and Renault models – a ping-pong ball, coffee-cup handles, a shock absorber. The result was *Baboon With Young* (1951), one of Picasso's most successful metamorphoses.

A gas tap for the crest, a shovel for the back, and two forks for the feet and the result was *The Crane* (1951); a stove, pie pans, and pipes make up *The Woman With the Pushchair* (1950), Picasso's first group work in the field of sculpture. Wicker basket, ceramic pots, palm leaf, metal, wood, cardboard: the result was *The Goat* (1950).

Baboon With Young
1951
Plaster original (pottery, two
model cars, metal and plaster)
56 x 34 x 71
Musée Picasso, Paris
Photo RMN/B. Hatala, Paris

(following page)
"The Goat" in progress
in the studio, Vallauris
1950
Photo Chevojon
Musée Picasso, Paris
Photo RMN/F. Raux, Paris

"I start with the basket and arrive at the thorax, I go from metaphor to reality. I make this reality tangible, by using the metaphor in this way. And even if the symbol is commonplace, I use it even if it's tattered in such an unexpected way that I create a new emotion in the spectator's mind[19]."

Little Girl Skipping (1950), made out of a wicker basket, a cake mould, a box of chocolate, shoes, wood, iron, pottery and plaster, then cast in bronze, expressed another artistic challenge – weightlessness – and fulfilled Picasso's wish "who had always dreamed of a sculpture that did not touch the ground": the ends of the rope hold up the girl who is nonchalantly jumping in the air. With the *Bathers*, Picasso confronts for the first time the problem of a group composed of several figures – *The Diver*, *The Man With Joined Hands*, *The Man-Fountain*, *The Child*, *The Woman With Outstretched Arms*, *The Young Man* – which function in synergy while retaining their own personality. The importance Picasso gave this group of figures originally made out of wood – planks, broomhandles, footboards, etc. – is evident given their appearance in the drawings and paintings for the decoration of the UNESCO building in Paris in 1957-1958.

19. Françoise Gilot, Carlton Lake, *Vivre avec Picasso*, Paris, Calmann-Lévy, 1964. (English trans.: *Life With Picasso*, Harmondsworth, Middx, Penguin, 1966).

"Pregnant Woman"
and "Little Girl Skipping"
Anonymous photograph
Musée Picasso, Paris
Photo RMN/F. Raux, Paris

Little Girl Skipping
1950
Bronze
152 x 65 x 66
Centre Pompidou, Mnam-Cci,
Paris

The Woman With Key, 1954, nicknamed *The Brothelkeeper*, is the product of pure improvisation. Made entirely out of elements found at hand (clay pipes, bricks), it is different from the others in that it is strictly an assemblage, not a combination of an assemblage and modeling. Its interpretation is a source of controversy due to its nickname, which refers to a woman running a brothel, a surprising choice given that Picasso did not return to this theme until the 1960s. Is the key the source of confusion, since it was an essential element in the sexual symbolism of the *Bathers* of the 1920s?

From 1951 to 1953, Picasso reintroduced painting into his sculpture when he made *Goat's Skull, Bottle and Candle*, which constitutes a transition toward the last phase of his artistic creativity. An entire series of paintings corresponds to this work either as an introduction or as a counterpart. The perpetual dialogue between painting and sculpture pursued since Cubism culminated in the 1960s in the variations on Manet's *Déjeuner sur l'herbe*. Color contributes to the intensification of the composition's expressiveness. Werner Spies saw in them the climax of Picasso's plastic resources: "The bottle evokes the problem of an open-ended, transparent sculpture, as is the case with *Glass of Absinthe*; the metal framework integrated into the bottle to suggest volume calls to mind the metal pieces executed with González; the children's bicycle's handlebars which constitute the goat's horns evoke the *Head of a Bull*. Small nails form the crown of hairs between the goat's horns while bigger nails create the candlelight; as for the surface of the skull, obtained by the imprint of corrugated cardboard on plaster, it goes back to the first use of structures that replaced modeling. The eyes, finally, are metal bolts[20]."

20. Werner Spies, *Picasso sculpteur*, Ostfildern, Hatje-Cantz, 2000.

**Picasso in Vallauris
with "The Woman With Key"
("The Brothelkeeper")**
1954-1957
Photo Edward Quinn
Musée Picasso, Paris
Photo RMN, Paris

Paint accentuates the character of the sculpture made out of two antagonistic blocks which seem to turn like a propellor, and a compact and stable structure, the skull; the composition offers us once again a *memento mori* opposing death, symbolized by the goat skull, and life, symbolized by the shining candelight evoking man's procreating energy. As for the bottle, it plays an essential role because it inaugurates an extremely dense sequence of folded sheet-iron works, for which he made scale models or paper or cardboard patterns which an artisan then carved out in sheet-iron for him. The sheet-iron sculptures, *The Chair* or *Pregnant Woman*, give a startling impression of nimbleness, because the sheet-iron painted white is indeed easily assimilated with a sheet of paper and offers a multiplicity of angles of vision, obtained through folding, and which brings the Cubist adventure to a close; the black and white or color intervene to express Picasso's sentiment: in order to obtain a sculpture, one needs only to cut up a painting. He added: "They end up being things that I keep. A chair. It is, basically, the laboratory, things from the laboratory[21]."

21. Radio interview with Picasso by Jean d'Alvez, *op. cit.*

The Chair
1961, Cannes
Cut-out, folded and painted sheet-iron
111.5 x 114.5 x 89
Musée Picasso, Paris
Photo RMN/B. Hatala, Paris

(following pages)
Picasso setting figures around "Head of a Woman"
1957
Photo David Douglas Duncan
Musée Picasso, Paris
Photo RMN, Paris

Jacqueline With a Green Ribbon
1962, Mougins
Sheet-iron with oil paint and crayon
50.7 x 39 x 28
Courtesy Jan Krugier, Dittesheim & Co, Geneva

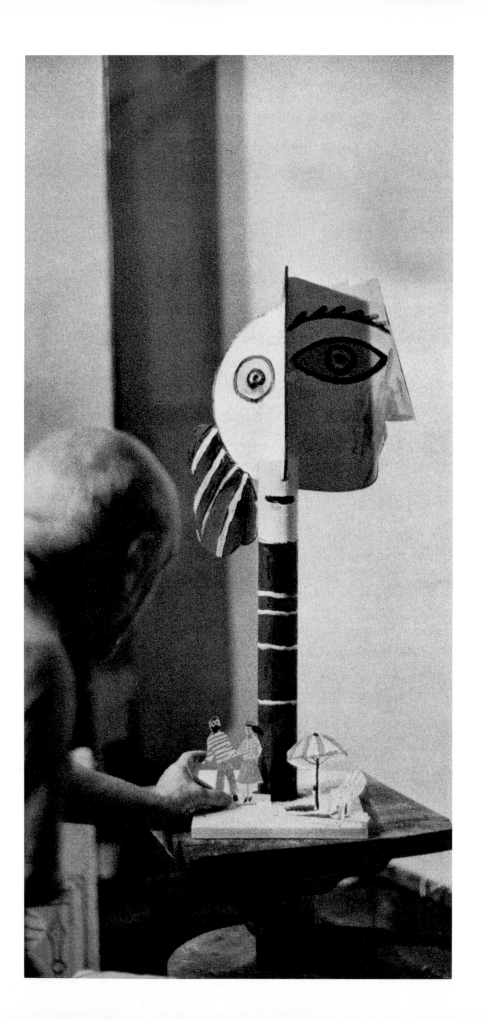

While working in sheet-iron, he had the opportunity of working in the monumental format he had always dreamed of, thanks to the Swedish sculptor Carl Nesjar, who was using a technique developed in Oslo called "betograve". This process permitted the engraving of a drawing through a spray of sand on a cement surface, and Picasso asked Nesjar to pursue these experiments with black and white gravel. The Picasso/Nesjar collaboration began in 1957 and allowed for the enlargement of the folded paper and cardboard scale models drawn in pencil of the *Déjeuner sur l'Herbe* series. The paper scale model depicting a female head for a sculpture twenty meters high destined to be placed in front of the Chicago Civic Center was made in Corten stainless steel and takes up the concept of the interplay of projections and hollows. After 1962, Picasso stopped working with sculpture. Over the course of the sixty years devoted to this discipline, he had produced a collection of works filled with imagination, innovation and fantasy, which, more than any other, sums up, by itself, the art of our century.

Dominique Dupuis-Labbé
(English translation by Liz Ayre and Jerome Reese)

**Head (Model for
The Chicago Civic Center)**
1962-1964, Mougins
Cut-out sheet-iron
105 x 70 x 48
Private collection
Courtesy Jan Krugier, Dittesheim
& Co, Geneva

chronology of Picasso's sculpture

1900 Picasso's first trip to Paris. He visits the International Exhibition pavilion displaying Rodin's works.

1902 In Barcelona, he asks sculptor Emili Fontbona to teach him how to model clay. *Sitting Woman* is the first sculpture he does in clay. Two other sculptures are done in bronze.

April 1904 At Ambroise Vollard's, Picasso discovers the sculptures which Gauguin sent from the Marquesas Islands.

Spring 1905 Rodin retrospective at the Salon du Luxembourg.

Picasso does *The Jester*, sculpted in wax using techniques similar to those which Degas used.

Winter 1905-1906 Presentation at the Louvre of recently excavated archaic Iberian sculptures.

Early 1906 Gauguin's influence – ever more concision, smooth surface, no impact of light on sculpture – appears in *Head of Fernande*, modeled after his companion's head, probably in Paco Durio's atelier who has been a collector and admirer of Gauguin since 1894.

Summer 1906 After a trip to Barcelona, Picasso leaves for Gósol with Fernande. Here, he sculpts primitive forms in boxwood: *The Nude With Raised Arms*, *Female Bust (Fernande)*, which he embellishes with paint. The work opens new perspectives for him. He executed many preliminary drawings for the groundbreaking *Portrait of Gertrude Stein*, which moved him closer to Cubism.

Autumn 1906 Back in Paris, Picasso learns from Durio how to work with sandstone, reinforcing his link with Gauguin even further.

Julio González
in his studio in Arcueil with
"Woman With a Mirror"
1937
Photo Rogi-André
Julio González Archives, IVAM,
Valencia

1907 Picasso moves more and more toward a greater simplification of forms: Figure (Werner Spies, *Picasso sculpteur*, Ostfildern, Hatje-Cantz, 2000, n° 15 and n° 19).

Autumn 1909 The culminating point of this period is the great Cubist *Female Head (Fernande)*, first done in plaster in the atelier of sculptor Manolo. Picasso is distancing himself from Durio's aesthetic approach.

1912 Picasso begins to explore Cubism, having worked intensely in painting since autumn 1906. In late 1912, he

introduces sculpted objects by using cardboard cutouts, string, wire, *papier collé* and other elements. *Guitars* and *Violins* are created, to be hung on the wall. He works on these until 1926.

Spring 1914 The six different versions of *Glass of Absinthe*, each painted in the different

colors Picasso uses for bronzes, are part of his movement into Synthetic Cubism.

1928 Christian Zervos publishes "Sculptures of Painters Today", *Cahiers d'art* (VII), with eight sculptures by Picasso, including Cubist constructions. Picasso sculpts *Metamorphoses I* and *II* after drawings executed the previous year reproduced in *Cahiers d'art*. In March, he works again with sculptor Julio González. Impressed by the dexterity of the Catalan artist, Picasso imagines having him execute the models and drawings he him-

self has done: *Head* (Spies 66) and the four versions of the *Monument to Apollinaire*. González has the locale, tools and skill; Picasso wants to employ them for an assemblage of a monumental sculpture: *The Woman in the Garden*.

1930-1934 The Château de Boisgeloup, near Gisors, is purchased. Picasso begins work at Boisgeloup on a series of plaster sculptures, most of which will be cast in bronze a few years later. An exhibition is held for the eight pine sculptures, Galerie des Cahiers d'Art, in June 1936

Chest and Head(s)
of Women
Anonymous photograph
Musée Picasso, Paris
Photo RMN/F. Raux, Paris

Dolls (Paloma)
1953 (from a set of seven)
Painted wood
Private collection

(article by González in *Cahiers d'art*, January 1937).

1932 Galeries Georges Petit, first retrospective of Picasso's works: seven sculpted works (four versions done by Vollard of the early sculptures, three by González of the metal sculptures) but no Cubist sculptures. Summer at Boisgeloup with Marie-Thérèse.

1934 *Woman With Foliage* (Spies 157) and *The Woman With the Orange* (Spies 236).

August 1936 Picasso, accompanied by Paul Eluard, discovers Vallauris, which has been a pottery village since Antiquity. In the autumn, Picasso – who is obliged to leave Boisgeloup after separating from his wife – works in a studio which Vollard lends him in Le Tremblay-sur-Mauldre, with Marie-Thérèse and their daughter Maya.

July 12, 1937 Inauguration of the Spanish pavilion at the Paris International Exhibition. Along with *Guernica*, two sculptures are presented: a *Female Head* from 1931 (Spies 133) and *Woman With Vase* from 1933 (Spies 135).

1941 *Female Head* (Dora Maar) in plaster (Spies 197).

Spring 1942 *Head of a Bull*: assemblage (Spies 240).

1943 Picasso undertakes a series of drawings on *Man With a Sheep* theme in July 1942, then executes a version in clay with an iron armature in February-March 1943, as with *Death's Head* (Spies 219), which is later cast in bronze.

1944 In May, Brassaï begins to photograph Picasso's bronzes, which are housed in the atelier on Rue des Grands-Augustins. On October 6,

Picasso presents five recently executed sculptures at the Salon de la Libération.

April 12-May 12, 1945 The Denver Art Museum holds the exhibition "Picasso: Paintings, Sculpture and Drawings".

July 26, 1946 While staying with the Ramiés, Picasso begins to experiment with ceramics at the Madoura studio, a pottery studio in Vallauris. He sculpts two bulls and a faun in clay.

1948 *Les Sculptures de Picasso* is published by Daniel-Henry Kahnweiler (Éditions du Chêne), with photographs by Brassaï taken at Boisgeloup or Rue des Grands-Augustins.

November 26, 1948 - late May 1949 The Maison de la Pensée française exhibits 149 of Picasso's ceramics and the sculpture *Man With a Sheep*. In the spring, Picasso returns to Vallauris, rents some old pottery warehouses on Rue

1950 Françoise Gilot gives birth to Paloma on April 19, 1949. The second version of *Pregnant Woman* is cast in bronze in 1959. Picasso executes a series of sculptures at Vallauris: *Little Girl Skipping*, *The Woman With the Pushchair* and *The Goat*.

From January 24 to March 19, the Museum of Modern Art of New York presents "Picasso: the Sculptor's Studio". The text of the catalogue is by William S. Lieberman. When the weather turns good, assemblages of objects are found in the areas surrounding Vallauris. On August 6, a copy of *Man With a Sheep* is

du Fournas and sets up three studios: one for painting, one for sculpture and one for ceramics. In the autumn, Picasso actively begins to sculpt again, and does a series of small fauns and centaurs, *Pregnant Woman* (Spies 347).

installed on the Place de Vallauris.

November 1950 - June 1951 The Maison de la Pensée française presents "Picasso, Sculptures, Drawings". Aragon writes the preface to the catalogue. *Man With a Sheep* is again displayed with its preliminary sketches.

October 1951 *Baboon With Young* (Spies 463), *Watering Can With Flowers* (Spies 239); *Goat's Skull, Bottle and Candle* (Spies 410).

Vase: Woman With a Mantilla
1949
White body; thrown and modeled; painted with slips
47 x 12.5 x 9.5
Musée Picasso, Paris
Photo RMN/G. Blot, Paris

Picasso with a Bather: The Child
1956
Photo Edward Quinn
Musée Picasso, Paris
Photo RMN, Paris

October 1954 *The Woman With Key.*

1956-1965 Picasso encounters Nesjar. Nesjar shows him photos of his projections on concrete. Picasso has new perspectives for participating in works exhibited for the city. Using the "beto-grave" technique, Picasso executed monumental sculptures in France, Barcelona, the United States and Scandinavia from scale models until 1965.

Colette Giraudon

**Centre national d'art
et de culture
Georges Pompidou,
Paris**

Jean-Jacques Aillagon
president

Guillaume Cerutti
director

Werner Spies
director of the Musée
national d'art moderne

curators of the exhibition

Werner Spies
director of the Musée
national d'art moderne,
Centre Pompidou

Dominique Dupuis-Labbé
curator at the Musée
national Picasso

The exhibition
is supported
by François Pinault,
Artémis President.

ARTEMIS

The exhibit is part of France's
official Year 2000 Celebration
program.

album

This album has been published in
conjunction with the exhibition
"Picasso sculpteur" on display at
the Centre Pompidou from June
8 to September 25, 2000

Editor
Dominique Dupuis-Labbé

Documentation
Sylvie Fresnault, Musée Picasso

Chronology
Colette Giraudon

English translation
Liz Ayre, Jerome Reese

Published in 2000 by Éditions du
Centre Pompidou. No part of
the content of this book may be
reproduced without the written
permission of the publisher.
© Succession Picasso,
Paris, 2000
© Estate Brassaï

Design
(L)**design**, Stéphanie Chavanon

**Éditions
du Centre Pompidou**

Director
Martin Bethenod

Associate director
Philippe Bidaine

Editorial Manager
Françoise Marquet

Editorial Coordinator
Dominique Moyen

Production Manager
Martial Lhuillery

Public relations
Danièle Alers

© Éditions du Centre Pompidou,
Paris, 2000

French edition ISBN
2-84426-046-2
English language edition ISBN
2-84426-073-X
N° d'éditeur 1136
Printed and bound in France
Legal deposit: June 2000